Emperor of Rome Julian

Historical Rrevelations of the Relation existing between Christianity and Paganism since the Disintegration of the Roman Empire

Emperor of Rome Julian

Historical Rrevelations of the Relation existing between Christianity and Paganism since the Disintegration of the Roman Empire

ISBN/EAN: 9783743308244

Manufactured in Europe, USA, Canada, Australia, Japa

Cover: Foto ©Thomas Meinert / pixelio.de

Manufactured and distributed by brebook publishing software (www.brebook.com)

Emperor of Rome Julian

Historical Rrevelations of the Relation existing between Christianity and Paganism since the Disintegration of the Roman Empire

HISTORICAL REVELATIONS

OF THE RELATION EXISTING BETWEEN

CHRISTIANITY AND PAGANISM

SINCE THE

Disintegration of the Roman Empire.

BY THE

ROMAN EMPEROR JULIAN

BOSTON:

COLBY & RICH, PUBLISHERS,

Corner Bosworth and Province Streets.

1886.

T. C. BUDDINGTON'S

(The Medium)

STATEMENT.

———•———

THE question of obtaining accurate information from the chief actors in the historic realm has long been of great interest to me. Earthly history has always seemed to be deficient from its inability to record only the external acts; whereas the subtle forces which produce external acts seemed to be overlooked by the earthly historian, or, if understood, are passed by in silence.

Causation in the realm of history, like causation in the sphere of physical forces, must be studied; and it seems to be the province of this work to inform the world of some of the true causes which have made modern civilization such a combination of heterogeneous materials.

The personal influence of the spirit, purporting to be Julian, is of the most pure and elevated character. There has never been a trace (discernable, at least) of any motive save to express in our language the

(3)

true status of his own earthly career, with the influence which, in after years, obscured the truth, and involved the world in mental darkness for a thousand years.

It seems to be essential to all lovers of pure truth that such minds as those in accord with Julian, upon the spirit side of life, should have free access to this life ere there can be any very valuable ideas transmitted from the spirits. If this class of spirits can come to aid us in our pursuit of a knowledge of the truth, we shall be likely to have that type of thought which, if different from ordinary so-called spirit communications, may be as instructive and valuable in their special department as the latter.

The time seems to be ripe for this class of influences to be invited to contribute of their knowledge to our incomplete records; and, if mediumship has any value, it should be exercised where light is most needed.

INTRODUCTION.

IT may seem to be an impossibility to the mortal mind for one who has been so long a resident in the world of spirit to be able to accurately convey to minds upon the earth sphere true ideas concerning his own age, and their relationship to the thoughts prevalent in succeeding ages.

But if you will consider that the mental nature never ceases to exist, and its action is such that no experience is ever entirely forgotten, you can see that all that is required for the transmission of the ideas to the earthly side is a properly-constructed brain, to act as a registering-battery, and any idea ever held by any mind can be recorded in language intelligible to mortals, for language is only the vehicle for transmission of ideas upon the earthly plane.

There is a link in the chain of ideas which binds me to the earth sphere, because my work there was prematurely shortened by my sudden transition at a period fraught with great interest to the world.

The revolutionary policy of Constantine, combined with the decay of polytheism, demanded the exercise of the wisest discretion in dealing with the new conditions of public affairs, and upon me, above others, devolved the responsibility of arresting the tendency of the national life towards destruction.

I was deprived of the opportunity to transfer the public attention from the influences of the old *régime* to the new policy by my death. My successors having been duly deprived of the exercise of private judgment through the craft of their priestly instructors let the Empire drift to destruction.

The unscrupulous zeal with which my memory has been assailed creates a desire upon my part to return, and, through the only means at my disposal, correct the errors prevalent among mortals concerning my life on earth.

I loved the truth, and reveled in the highest delights of exaltation while on earth, having the company of the wise and enlightened for counselors, and have never regretted the change of teachers which my thirst for knowledge instituted.

Well would it have been for the world if I had succeeded in substituting the reign of philosophy and reason for religious dogmatism in that age; and better yet will it be if the world should ever be emancipated from all the slavish superstitions of the past through love of truth, and obedience to its mandates.

JULIAN.

CHAPTER I.

THE POLITICAL STATUS OF THE EMPIRE.

I⊤ is with no feelings of acrimony or bitterness that I come back to the sphere of mortal thought, but rather to illuminate the profoundly darkened record of the ideas of my age. I was known as the Emperor Julian,—one whose name has been equally lauded for philosophic elevation of character, and condemned for apostacy to the religion of his youth.

It is not my purpose to retrace the successive steps of calumny and malignant zeal whereby the light and glory of ancient philosophic truths were deliberately obscured, and in their place the standards of bigoted ignorance and credulity erected. The time is ripe for the world to know the truth about that period of its history, when the prestige of Grecian philosophy was at its highest development.

The Empire, for the first two centuries of the so-called Christian era, was not the prey of the seditious and destructive elements of human society, as history asserts; but, with few exceptions, its emperors were men of liberal and advanced ideas of human progress, and sought the welfare of their subjects and the

Empire, although in so doing they depended upon the military resources too much for the ultimate good of the people.

It is not true, however, that a spirit of war for the sake of conquest was the ruling motive of the national character, although you, who read the history of that period, might justly think so. It was the purpose of Rome to bring all nations upon a basis of international security for individuals, and to be a Roman citizen carried with it the prerogative of protection from injustice greater than that possessed by its titled officials.

The ægis of protection being thrown over conquered nations, enabled civilization to press forward with strides that were impossible among the isolated tribes and principalities, which, previous to their incorporation in the Empire, regarded strangers as enemies.

It was the mission of imperial Rome to make civilized intercourse a possibility, where before intercourse was regarded as the precursor of invasion and destruction. Independence in tribal relations was the basis of political liberty; but independence without cohesive union or confederation was the chief cause of barbaric isolation. Nations have distinct relations to human progress. They arise in obedience to specific demands of the epochs in which they exist and flourish. They are not without definite and necessary functions in the sphere of human advancement, and whenever they are acting in accordance with their natural relations to the race, they flourish and become great and powerful.

Rome, under a republican form of government, consolidated and civilized the barbaric hordes of Western Europe, changing them from a host of warring tribes into the founders of the most powerful nations upon the earth existing at the present age. She did this by recognition of the principle of incorporating all countries which submitted to her sway as equals before the common law, and was the first nation of any great importance, in that age, which practically adopted the wisdom of Grecian philosophy in constructing a national government.

Under this principle, despotic or arbitrary power upon the part of any ruler was attended with danger and disgrace, and could not be enforced for any great length of time.

The change from the Republic to the Empire was not, as first appears, a retrogressive step, but was the result of the overwhelming preponderance of the military power, which sought relief from anarchy through centralization. I regard it as the legitimate fruits of the extension of the Empire toward the East, and the attempt to apply the same principles to nations civilized under despotic rulers which were found so successful in dealing with the barbarous hordes of the North.

The introduction of Persian civilization created a disposition to utilize the military strength in conquests for personal glory, and the subtlety of the Oriental character demanded a different exhibition of force than that held and exerted by the consuls, who could be suspended or degraded by the Roman Senate.

It was this inadaptability of the Republic to deal
with and incorporate into the body politic the nations
of Asia that swayed the mind of Julius Cæsar to turn
his arms against the old *régime*, and center the power
where it could successfully deal with the problems
of Asiatic civilization. Julius never sought imperial
power, because he was at heart a tyrant. In fact, he
foresaw the evils as well as benefits that might, and
probably would, result in a change; but he also saw
that in order to conserve the fruits of victory, the
time was ripe for the nation to stretch its arm over
the East, clothed with a power that the people of
that type of civilization would respect and understand; and as there was nothing more to gain in
Europe, he turned his arms against his old colleagues,
and overthrew all that would or could prevent the
full exercise of the Roman laws in the eastern part
of the Empire.

The practical effect of the change was beneficial
to the eastern world. For the first time since the
Assyrian Empire existed despotic power was exercised
in behalf of human welfare, for Cæsar never changed
the civil code, except in adding to it the supreme
power of Imperator, and under that title compelled
the civil codes of the provinces to conform to that of
Rome.

ROME.

All nations have what may be termed specific
periods of vitality, arising from concentration of the
mental power of the people upon definite lines of
action. The Roman yoke — while foreign in name
to the people of the Orient — nevertheless com-

mended itself to the philosophic thought of the enlightened, for it made personal liberty of conscience inviolate, and, in so doing, enabled the thinking mind to fearlessly expand under the protection of the civil law.

The recognition of all gods as equally worthy of adoration was the germ of that phase of religious toleration which, at the present time, emancipates the mind from a superstitious fear of any, and in that one principle alone is found the greatest factor in mental exaltation.

My own history — as given to the world by the superstitious devotees of a mistaken interpretation of the old mysteries — is replete with errors which base minds always attribute to those whose mental status is in advance of their own. I was not a superstitious devotee of the pagan gods, nor did I strive to reinstate their worship among the people, as essential to a true conception of religious duties; but I sought to elevate the populace above a superstitious regard for any human deity, and in partaking of the ceremonial observances I made no distinction in the rites for each and all, thereby hoping to express to the people my estimate of the folly of attaching much importance to the powers of any.

My traducers, however, took good care to obliterate this view from history, and with undue acrimony recorded what was really a philosophic satire upon themselves as a proof of a deep-seated purpose to restore, in its ancient splendor, the worship of deities who had become obsolete through a better understanding of the truth among the enlightened.

My civil policy was for the restoration of the philosophic ideas which had made the Empire so powerful
under the early emperors. Under the wretched management of some of the later emperors justice and
equality had departed from the representatives of the
civil code, which made anything like unity of purpose
among the different provinces an impossibility. The
people no longer came to the support of the national
power, and rebellion against it arose in all quarters,
chiefly because it no longer commanded respect, from
its disregard of justice expressed by its subordinate
officers.

Under the sway of military force a semblance of
national unity indeed existed, but it was by the force
of compulsion, not attraction. I sought to substitute for this the principles of equity and justice, and,
had my life been spared, might have done something
to have delayed the process whereby the Empire
swiftly hastened to its destruction.

I foresaw, from a knowledge of the overthrow of
the old Greek republic, that the nation, however
powerful in external appearance, could not long
remain intact with internal dissension preying upon
its vitals, and also understood well the policy of
Constantine and his sons to avert the forthcoming
dissolution of the Empire. They adopted the mistaken policy of force and treachery in dealing with
the just claims of the populace, and sought by violence to establish the imperial power upon a basis of
despotic authority, although thereby alienating the
good will of the enlightened and influential portion
of their subjects.

I strove to reinstate the old policy of justice and equality, and can truly say that, although my life was often in danger from the jealousy of my relations, yet never did a subject of mine (once understanding the motives of my reign) think of raising the standard of revolt against me. I was compelled by the affection of my soldiers to assume the purple, when nothing but a hope and wish for the ability to exercise the imperial power for the benefit of the people would have tempted me, for a moment, from the exercise of the pursuits of study and philosophy. It was a vain attempt upon my part. But it was the only policy that could have averted the fate which afterwards befell the Empire.

The Christian priesthood at Rome, and throughout the Empire, were, even then, plotting the destruction of the civil power, and substituting for it the supremacy of ecclesiastical jurisdiction over the race.

It was one of those peculiar phases of mental obscuration that naturally follow from the too close observance of one range of ideas. And the subordination of everything in the Empire to the military power paved the way for the subjection of the civil code to the ecclesiastical claims for universal dominion.

I do not think there would have been any possible chance for the overthrow of the imperial power had the later emperors of the third century been faithful to the principles of the old laws. But they had abandoned many of the most essential features of the old national policy, and the artful influence of the Christian priesthood made it comparatively easy to change the current of national prosperity into the dark channels of shame and degradation.

Constantine sought to restore the traditional splendor of the Augustan age, but failed in the effort to perpetuate that regard for the nation which is the only basis of true prosperity; for, by the admission of the Christian priesthood to a controlling influence in shaping the education of the youth, he submitted at the most critical period of mental activity the plastic mind of youth to the influence of superstition and intrigue in place of the lofty thoughts and ideals of the Platonic philosophy.

Christian superstition sought to enforce its tenets upon the mind through suppressive action of the intellectual faculties, by insisting upon belief in authority as superior to the effect of inquiry and investigation; and although the priesthood of the old religions had asserted the existence and supremacy of the gods, it had never assumed to transcend the teachings of philosophy by its oracles; for, in fact, the oracles were but the methods whereby the philosophy of past ages was enshrined and understood in its deepest significance.

There were, however, efforts made during the period preceding Constantine to consolidate priestly authority with the civil power; but it was during his reign and his immediate successor when the greatest effort was made to substitute sacerdotal officers as the best instructors for the youth,— a policy I saw and felt to be fraught with destructive tendencies to both truth and the Empire. Hence, I instituted a different policy; for I saw that the philosophic schools were safer auxiliaries to the true national welfare than the Christian priesthood, inasmuch as they placed a higher estimate upon the growth of moral power in the individual than a desire for conquest and personal aggrandisement.

CHAPTER II.

THE records of the old Roman Empire are replete with instruction to the student of political forces. They have been mutilated and falsified to such a degree that the present age fails to comprehend in scarcely any degree the real influence and power that epoch in history has had in shaping the governing powers of modern civilization.

The great results which have arisen from the adoption of the political status of that period are seen in the acknowledgment of individual rights, irrespective of creed, race, or religion. Rome, under the Cæsars, gave the world the supremacy of the civil law against the machinations of craft and ambition, —either in religion or autocracy. Externally, it does not appear to have done so. But as long as knowledge of the truth is diffused, it will be perceived that Roman civilization was based upon the principles of equality of all before the law. And no immunity from just penalty for transgressions was withheld from emperor or peasant without a defiance of law, which, if exerted by the ruling power, generally resulted in assassination. I do not mean by this that individual transgressions of the civil policy by certain emperors were not sometimes condoned; but never, for the first two centuries, did any emperor fail to receive just punishment who deliberately sought to annul the great principle of Roman citizenship,— a principle that was supreme in the constitution of the government.

It was here that the only great question of policy arose, when Julius Cæsar transferred the imperial power from the senate to the throne; and as long as the throne respected it, it in turn supported the imperial executive.

It was never contemplated by the advocates of imperialism to establish a despotism; and Julius himself, although ambitious to wield imperial power, sought only to use it in behalf of the old national policy. His assassination was one of those blunders that are worse than crimes; for, with the exception of Brutus, no other conspirator enlisted in that enterprise who would not have established autocratic authority had he been in Julius's position. Julius sought to avert the disintegration of the Republic into factions that would have been mutually destructive, and, in destroying each other, obliterated the sentiment of human responsibility for crime.

His act preserved the nation from premature dismemberment, and, at the same time, gave the illiterate hordes of the West the refining influence of the East, without destroying the independent disposition which has ever since marked the civilization of Europe.

In the transition from the barbarian condition to civilization, the European character became subject to no influence for evil until after the age of Constantine, but rather rose steadily from its state of traditional savagery toward that of semi-civilization. Its people were stern and self-reliant, furnishing the best of material for a conquering soldiery, and yet holding the love of honor, and regard for honor, as prime factors of character. They were a worthy race to absorb the old principles of the Republic, and interweave them in the solid character which marks the German and Briton of the present age.

THE RELIGIOUS STATUS.

No history of the Empire which conceals or ignores the true state of religious thought during my age is worthy of trust or consideration. Therefore I deem it necessary to write more explicitly upon that subject than upon the merely military or civil status.

The religious ideas of the Empire were a crude mass of ill-digested absurdities. The western mythology had its votaries in the soldiery, drawn from the regions of Spain, Gaul, and Germany, who brought to the eastern provinces the crude legends of their own nations. The transferral of the legions from one province to another served to introduce the peculiar ideas of each section, for in the wake of the army followed priest and proselyter of the ruling power.

This process of intermingling of nations was the

policy adopted by the Empire to prevent insurrection, and without that as a preliminary Christian faith could not have been as successful as it was in becoming known to such a vast number in so short a period.

I do not think that the Christian emperors ever realized the true reason for such a widespread acceptance of the Christian faith; but it seems to me to have originated in the disposition of the masses to curry favor with the ruling power.

As long as the pagan emperors controlled the destinies of the Empire no special effort was made to substitute the worship of Jupiter for that of Thor, Odin, or other gods; but the inevitable effect of military success was to pave the way for the priests of all faiths to compare and council together.

When the Empire had made interchange of religious ideas possible, and protected the worshipers of all gods equally, the immediate result was — not as might be supposed — jealousy and contention, but combination, and, where possible, substitution of the ideas nearest to those held by the civil power.

It was the constant aim of the Christian priesthood to unify the religions of the Empire, and never were efforts more persistently made by any class of minds to combine the same essential ideas in all religions in one than were made by them.

There was a fanatical impulse from the spiritual world itself which facilitated this; for some of the more ambitious minds in spirit life thought that a great good to the race might result from the establishment of a uniform standard rather than from such diversity as had formerly prevailed, and through psychological impressions carried their dupes to the utmost bounds of the Empire, and even beyond them, in their zeal to effect what nature has made an impossibility. Hence, although the efforts were nominally successful in many instances, the real result was to retard mental growth among those peoples who were unfitted by their birth and surroundings to accept such ideas in their true significance. With their success developed a love of power, which increased to such an extent as to control the civil power; and, by virtue of invisibility, it held a tremendous influence in mortal life through the ignorance there concerning it. It was the transposal of the old oracular power which was once regarded as advisory only to that of an arbitrary, invisible autocracy, and with more terrible results to mortals than ever was possible under the old pagan *régime*.

CHAPTER III.

As the history of the western Empire is chiefly a
record of ecclesiastical triumphs, it necessitates a
chapter, or series of chapters, upon the efforts of the
civil power to recover its rightful position in the relations of human rights to priestly assumption.

The importance of the work of the minds of
past ages in shaping the thought of the present cannot be estimated by those in mortal life. As the
tree is known by its fruits, so does the mental bias
of early teachings produce that condition (mental
peculiarity) which makes criminality of action seem
to be just and expedient.

Constantine the Great was subject from his earliest recollection to scenes of blood and violence. His
mother was a woman of unscrupulous ambition, without moral restraint, and she duly instilled in his
youthful mind the base motives which actuated her-
self, and coupled with her great influence was the
crafty policy of Eusebius, whose character was without honesty, or regard for truth.

I knew well the hatred and dissimulation that were the governing motives of that family, and how little I had to hope from them, if I had desired to participate in the political relations which embroiled the rest of my family, and so chose to devote myself to the pursuits of science and philosophy. Eusebius was governed by the motive of establishing his own fame in literature, and, in order to do this, catered to the prejudices of Constantine, promising him to so record his deeds, as a monarch, as to give posterity a great regard for the events of his age. Constantine was so desirous of appearing to posterity as the equal of Augustus that he transferred the seat of government to Byzantium, and sought to emulate the history of Julius as the founder of a new *régime* which should combine the splendor of the East with the power of the West.

The transfer of the capital to Byzantium left the West at the mercy of ecclesiastical power, which was unscrupulously exerted to pave the way for a general transferral of authority from the civil to the religious order, and thereby overthrow the policy which had enabled Rome, under the first emperors, to successfully conserve and extend the power of the Republic.

I think the ecclesiastical history of Eusebius was intended by him to help produce this result, although he himself did not realize nor imagine that it would, or could, be accomplished in so short a space of time. But herein must be considered the power of the spiritual realm which ever was exerting its influence upon the affairs of the nation.

From the earliest ages the mental power of such, in spirit life, as had arisen to an appreciation of the importance of truth and philosophy in the life of mortals was directed toward the perfection of conditions whereby the plastic mind could develop under the ideas of truth and justice.

They centered their power upon Rome, from its commanding position upon the Mediterranean, and developed first the military element which gave it success in war. They chose Rome to embody the great principle of equality before the law as a generic principle of national safety.

No nation could successfully contend with her; for, literally, the gods fought for her, and inspired her soldiery with immortal valor. She conquered and incorporated all as parts of the national body politic, obedient to this spiritual force which sought by her to overthrow autocratic authority or tribal anarchy. There was never any essential defeat to her arms as long as this spiritual force over her was recognized and obeyed; but from the time when Constantine and the priesthood, under Eusebius, sought to establish autocratic power through religion, using the force of the civil law to regulate and overthrow the ideas of the old philosophy, then the spiritual power which sought to preserve the civil supremacy was withdrawn, or rather could no longer exert its influence save to oppose the tendency of the age, and internal dissention took the place of the old spirit of co-operation and extension of the Empire.

Truly there was a spiritual force being exerted in

behalf of Constantine by the selfish and ambitious spirits who had reveled in similar scenes of blood and disorder. But they lacked the lofty aspirations of the old fathers of the nation, and also the wisdom whereby they could safely direct the affairs of the State from the dangers that beset it through their own disregard of true principles.

The old spiritual forces were, indeed, withdrawn; but not without struggles to reach the minds upon whom had fallen the nominal power, and occasionally they reached one or another; but never could they hold their influence sufficiently to restrain the madness which hurled the Empire to its ruin through the determination of the religious element to retain its power over the people through cultivating their superstitious nature.

If the statements of history regarding the life of the period of which I write were true, I should not care to attempt their refutation; but as I can see clearly the motives and results of these fictions, I feel like doing what I can to prevent their further influence upon the interests of the present age.

The great political force of Rome was not always seen, nor exemplified, by those who wore the purple, nor did the merely external pomp of the throne show the real purpose of its invisible supporters.

The populace were, indeed, placated for a time with the shows and spectacles of the arena; but the games and combats were really small factors in the governing principles of the Empire, though historians have given them so much importance. They reflected the ideas of military conquest which had become a

second nature to so many in the Empire by accustom-
ing the youth to scenes of blood and carnage, but
they were not upheld by the lovers of philosophy and
study, nor did they cease, or, rather, the principles
die, which made them possible when the Empire
changed from the pagan to the Christian faith.

The thirst for blood which, under the old reign,
was satisfied with the slaughter of beasts and criminals, under the new was satiated by the most cruel
tortures inflicted upon human beings for heresy; and
if the vilest criminals were spared the pangs of lace-
ration at the hands of each other, the most innocent,
and often praiseworthy, specimens of human culture
were forced prematurely from earthly life because of
their fidelity to truth.

The spirit of persecution and torture was never cherished nor exercised by the best philosophic thought
of my age any more than in yours, and the desire for
conquest, or exercise of power over others, is a sure
index of that type of development that made the
savage scenes of the arena a possibility in the age of
the Empire, or lighted the fires of the Inquisition in
the later period of fanaticism.

I would that I could correctly impress upon the
thought of the present age the true idea of intellectual and moral growth. It is not by the exercise of
arbitrary force over the will of the ignorant and erring, nor by cultivating the superstitious nature of
ignorant minds, but by asserting and demonstrating
the truth as nature, and the study of nature reveals
truth, that the race is elevated to a higher plane of
life.

The gods of Greece and Rome were misunderstood ideals. The God of Christian worship is an equally misunderstood ideal, taken from the best thought of speculative philosophy.

Had not the philosophy of Plato and Pythagoras permeated the thought of the Empire, Christian revelation would not, and could not, have obtained a footing, even with all the military and civil power at its command.

It was a compromise between the superstition of the past and the evolution of the future, and held its position by force, until the barbaric hordes of the North became sufficiently enlightened to substitute individual independence of thought, under the phrase "liberty of conscience," when its true nature became subject for the first time to intellectual scrutiny and criticism.

In the attempt of the priesthood, under Constantine, to change the type of religious thought, there was no apparent disposition to do more than embody the philosophic ideals of Platonism in the State religion. Secretly, there was a deep determination upon the part of its priesthood to utilize these ideals as a permanent power to modify and, as far as possible, overthrow the military spirit which had become too arbitrary in its policy towards individual rights; and had the Christian religion stopped here, it might have been a powerful factor in changing the destructive tendency of the military policy.

But it changed all that had made it co-operative with philosophy by its claims to arbitrary power over the soul, and in that one principle alienated the lovers of truth, allied to the military despotism the most aggravated form of mental tyranny, and when both became firmly seated on the throne, the mild and beneficent policy of Plato was swept into oblivion, and in its place darkness and desolation crept over the nations composing the old Empire, covering light and learning with a pall of errors through which feeble rays only could be perceived for more than a thousand years.

I do not wish you to think that in my endeavors to give you the truth about the mental state of the early Empire I make these charges against the mistaken devotees of Christianity, because they have recorded such false tales about the moral and religious status of the old Empire, or that Deity was so offended that he gave the ruling power into their hands whereby the temporal power of Rome was succeeded by the spiritual supremacy it has held since that age.

It was a natural result of a natural law which no ruler or policy could have prevented, unless he had changed the policy of the Empire at the time of Trajan in behalf of a universal republic, and brought the philosophy of Apollonius of Tyana, with the results of certain discoveries in science at Alexandria, to the aid of the nation. I think the time then was ripe for the co-operation of the wisest and best minds of the Empire to have so changed the national policy that the principle which you call "elective franchise" for the masses might have been safely adopted, and the nation not have been left subject to the will of a victorious, and often mercenary, soldiery.

I say, I think so; for at that time the great con

solidation of interests, which had been the policy of
Julius to effect, had been successfully accomplished;
and I am sure that then, if ever, would have been
the time for the people to have had a direct voice in
determining the choice of the executive.

If Roman civilization under the Empire was defective in some of its details, it certainly was far from
being what history — as transmitted by its defamers
— would seem to indicate. That such a nation could
arise, holding the position of general arbitrator of so
many diverse peoples without some great inherent
power, is so anomalous as to need no comment.
The great power of the Empire lay in its regard for
general principles which underlie human progress;
and it can truly be said that, under her pagan emperors, no nation was made any the worse who submitted to her yoke. Petty tyrants were compelled
to submit to the greater power, and the greater power
was too absorbed in providing for the contingencies
of the general welfare to pay attention to the trivial
demands of personal ambition.

It is the peculiar province of imperial power to be
instrumental in giving the masses a greater liberty
than possible under lesser governments, and as long
as the imperial power remained at Rome, undivided
in its exercise, the Empire flourished as it never did
after its removal to Byzantium. It was a mistake
for Constantine to have removed the seat of power,
for, in so doing, he lost the regard and support of
the western part of the Empire.

When the barbarian hordes of the North poured
down upon the doomed city, there was no incentive

upon the part of the people, who had been taught a servile dependance upon their priesthood, to turn back the tide of invasion; and that principle which, in the days of ancient Rome, had aroused the military ardor of every Roman to successful resistance was entirely wanting.

There can be no successful nationality which does not first find expression in obedience to the universal desire for self-preservation, and it is worthy of the attention of students of ancient history how supine and effeminate the nation of Rome became under the domination of the Christian priesthood. Beset and overthrown by barbarian and Christian, the prey of every enemy, her history for the past thousand years has been a striking contrast to that which she had under the pagan rule.

Cannot her Christian apologists see and understand that her fall was not from devotion to the pagan gods, but from her subservience to her Christian superstition?

Brennus met steel when he came, but Attila had gold only to vanquish his power. This was the difference between the type of manhood bred by the laws of the old faith and that encouraged by the new.

Roman manhood sank before the weight of a false regard for the claims of a false religion; but humanity suffered not less from the power and pangs of war.

The earth was stained with blood, shed in a vain strife for supremacy, without justice; and it is a striking comment upon the claims of the Christian

faith that it was not able to subvert the military
spirit among its believers; for the history of the old
Roman empire, since its division and overthrow, is a
series of bloody wars, in which personal liberty and
civil rights have been disregarded by each faction,
although the nations engaged in these wars professed
allegiance to the same religion, whose claims for
divine origin rests upon its devotion to the principles of universal brotherhood.

Christianity was never able to restrain the passions
of men from mutual slaughter, and it lacked the
fundamental power of enforcing its edicts by ignor-
ing the cultivation of the military spirit for the pres-
ervation of national life.   Hence, it could instigate
evil, but rarely could it promote the welfare of its
subjects in the practical details of life,— unlike the
old spirit of conquest which permeated the Empire
and welded the conquered nations into unity of purpose.

CHRISTIAN ROME DISINTEGRATED, THE EMPIRE AND
THE WORLD IS LEFT IN WORSE THAN EGYPTIAN
DARKNESS FOR MORE THAN A THOUSAND YEARS.

I look back over this period of the world's history
in astonishment, mingled with indignation, that such
an outcome could have followed the brilliant prom-
ise of the Empire during the first three centuries of
the Christian era.   Despite the corruption of the people, by the influence of Persian and Egyptian civilization, I believe that had Constantine and his successors kept the capital of the Empire in their grasp at
Rome, or, failing to appreciate its importance there,

had refused to permit the ecclesiastical power to usurp its functions, the western nations might have been held firm to their allegiance, and the world have had a different history.

The Empire of the West had all the elements of a mighty nationality which would, under central authority, based upon the old civil code, have given a civilization unstained with innocent blood, and capable of the highest degree of human progression. It came nearly to this condition after centuries of darkness, but not until the destructive features of the ecclesiastical power at Rome were discarded.

The failure to reach the high standard of national unity, which would have prevented war and enforced a true method of adjusting disturbances between the provinces, came from the loss of the military prestige which the Empire alone had with each section, and losing that hold, the nations of Europe have developed slowly, because of the absorption of so much force in jealousies and mutual antagonism.

For the people, born and bred under such conditions, there remains nothing but servility and long endurance of evils that breed riot and revolution at home, or an appeal to arms against fancied wrongs from neighboring kingdoms. The old remedy, which was popular at Rome for this state of feeling among the barbarian provinces, was the enlistment and occupation of the troops in foreign conquest, so that the balance of power was kept even between the people and the government.

IT IS NECESSARY TO REVERT TO THE THOUGHT OF
   PAST AGES IF ONE WOULD KNOW THE FULL SIG-
   NIFICANCE OF THE IDEAS OF THE PRESENT.

I can see clearly the mistaken policy of the Romish
Church in concealing the relations it holds to human
history, and why it is so strenuous for the survival
of its dogmas.

By this I mean *that the reconstructed paganism of
its creed* is the great obstacle to a true appreciation
of its mission in the world. Mary, as the mother of
Christ, and the spouse of Jehovah, is but another
version of the Egyptian and Hellenic ideas of the
divine relationship existing between creative power
and earthly results. *As a mythical tradition it does
no harm; but, taught as a sacred truth, it is the basis
of almost infinite error.*

The world of mortals is so subject to its delete-
rious influence that the bare description of its origin
is believed to be a shocking blasphemy, and the mental powers of otherwise well-educated minds are held
in abeyance through fear of it.

I would it were possible to delineate the whole
process whereby the transition of the pagan rites,
and the interpretation of the symbols, was accomplished; but that is a difficult task, owing to the
slow and secret methods utilized by the actors. It
was, however, upon nearly the same plane of action
whereby the ideas of the Christian church of the
present age are travestied in the creed and deeds of
the mob known as the "Salvation Army"; and if
you can imagine a great nation under the mental

influence of such a body of worshipers, you can get some idea of what power governed the masses of the church in the time of Constantine.

It was, indeed, a church militant, with the most responsible positions of educational and other equally important trusts in the hands of the ignorant, fanatical priesthood, which, having been elevated from the slums and gutters of the Empire under Constantine, sought by violence aud intrigue to maintain supremacy over the schools of Plato and Pythagoras.

I sought to change this by excluding such ignorance from controlling the destiny of a mighty empire, but in vain.

Do you wonder that some of us arise in wrath, and almost vengeance, when we behold the ruin and desolation wrought among the fairest lands of earth by the successful introduction and propagation of those old errors, and, through all available channels, seek to overthrow forever the power which still sits in imperial Rome fulminating edicts against the free exercise of the mind and conscience? When you realize that all that is really valuable in mortal or spirit life is the untrammeled development of the mind,— that spiritual growth is the outcome of a knowledge of truth, gained by experience or education,— then you will understand why we are so earnest about the propagation of truthful ideas upon earth, and the abandonment of all error by all minds. It is not against individual creeds that we wage this warfare, but against the false basis of the creed itself.

We know how difficult it is to change the type of

mentality when ignorance of the truth is its chief factor, and, therefore, are desirous

THAT INTELLIGENT IDEAS UPON ALL SUBJECTS SHOULD BE TAUGHT AND UNDERSTOOD BY MORTALS.

The primal ideas of the Christian faith are fictitious tales taken from the old myths. They were misunderstood by the Christian laity in my day, but were not unknown to the majority of the priesthood, and it has only been by their persistent reiteration as truth through succeeding ages that they have become permanent fixtures (in mortal life) among many nations. The tenacity with which the mind clings to the ideas, taught as truth in early life, is the great power by which these myths have become so strongly entrenched, and it is only by the continued efforts of the enlightened in both worlds to impress the truth about them upon the ignorant that there is any hope of ever lifting their influence from the myriad hosts who still believe in them as divine truths.

The myths (as of Mary and Jesus itself) are as groundless as that of Isis and Horus; let once the idea of either prevail as a divine revelation, and all the train of evil influences which secretly follow in the wake of each would again flood the nations with the fell results of vice and crime.

Truth has no need of rites and ceremonies, nor should it be veiled in secret mysteries. The mysteries themselves are nothing more than private

seances, with their necessary conditions for successful results.

The plain statement — that all oracles of the gods
and methods of divination were but the efforts of
spirits to reach mortals with certain ideas — is the
truth ; *and all else about the historical romances of the
gods are fictions of a corrupt priesthood to cover flagi-
tious crimes.*

CONTRASTS BETWEEN THE PAGAN AND CHRISTIAN PERSECUTION.

It has been the fashion with the Catholic hierarchy
to charge the Empire with permitting the worst forms
of licentiousness and vice to flourish under its pagan
rulers ; but little has ever been said by it about the
state of morals during the epoch of its Christian
emperors.

If the veil of hypocrisy which covers this period
should ever be lifted by those in the spirit world
cognizant of it, the world would cry out in horror
at the terrible sacrilege committed under apparent
approval of the appointed vicegerents of Christ.

Suffice it to say that so far from virtue being protected, and vice punished, the chiefest recommenda-
tion of the religion itself was in its promised immunity to the guilty from all punishment in either
world for the most heinous offenses, if committed in
behalf of the faith.

Pagan Rome never devised such tortures for the
worst criminals as did Christian Rome for innocent
heretics ; and never was blood shed more freely in
gladiatorial combats, for the populace to feast their

eyes upon, than flowed from the veins of those who were not even given a chance for safety by the reversal of the popular judgment.

I have witnessed scenes of cruelty in various portions of what was the Empire, since my transition, which would have appalled the stoutest warrior under the reigns of Galerius and Domitian, and have turned the edge of the sword of the former in behalf of the Christian victims who, guiltless of any crime, suffered the direst penalties that malice and baffled rage could inflict.

These martyrs to conviction of conscience are unrecorded upon the pages of worldly history; but they are not forgotten, and their power will yet be felt in undermining and overturning a religious system which made such deeds possible on earth.

Turn back the tide of a thousand years and behold the implements of torture which yet remain as mute witnesses of the type of character evolved under the policy of Augustine and Jerome. Think you that the apostate Julian would have permitted such a stain upon his name and character? Would Marcus Aurelius or even Domitian have been guilty of consigning human beings to the embrace of the Virgin? Answer, O Roman Pontiff, who sits upon their ruined throne, and see if ever again the Quirinal shall respond to the bidding of the Vatican!

Thou hadst thy time in full to transcend the record of the Cæsars; but thy page in history is so defiled with the blood of the innocent that in mercy to thy victims thy power to slay is taken from thee and placed in the hands of those who will never again permit it to be exercised on earth. It is not in thy power to stay the sword of justice which, at last, has overtaken thee. And if pagan Rome fell, as thou claimest, because of its disregard of human weal, thou, too, shalt not escape.

Know this: that those who once held the power over nations, which enabled thee to carry thy mandates to all peoples, have no less power in turning the course of empires whereby humanity shall escape thy present malevolence, and render all thy efforts to regain supremacy a nullity.

THE PHILOSOPHY OF NATIONAL LIFE.

The philosophy of civilization consists of keeping the balance of power between the conservative and progressive elements of society. This policy was the true course which Rome pursued among the barbarian hordes of the West, and the effeminate civilization of the East. She preserved the autonomy of her own State by carrying the principles of self-control among the nations she conquered, and elevating them as much as possible above the plane of despotic power. Her great mission was the introduction among nations of the principles of co-operation of forces in national aggrandisement.

In time she changed this policy for one of a different type, by introducing the arbitrary methods of the East, which occasioned the dissatisfaction among the provinces, and led to repeated rebellions.

I do not see how Rome could have been overthrown by any external force as long as she preserved the supremacy of the old civil code; but when that was surrendered to the power of ecclesiastical dictation, the national spirit departed from the heart of the populace, and disintegration rapidly ensued.

I know it has been said that nations must have their periods of growth and decay, like other productions of earth; but I now perceive that the *life principle of growth in nations is immortal* as in man, and no nationality need perish if it holds it intact.

Governments are overthrown when they cease to be imbued with this principle; and, when externally crushed by foreign powers, the true nation exists as long as the people will it to exist. Therefore, I say, that Rome might have stood to the present age under the power of just laws, and given to modern civilization the ripe fruits of generations of wisdom, while the terrible period of the dark ages never would have left its blight upon the pages of what should have been the brightest chapter in the record of ages.

From the hights of eternal wisdom we now see clearly the results of misdirected efforts, and the range of our vision takes in the vista of the world's past history, as yours would if it were emblazoned upon a gigantic panorama.

O Rome, thou mistress of the world! How are thou fallen from the high destiny foretold to Numa Pompilius! Thy boasted rule over all nations which many claim as its true fulfillment is thy deepest degradation; for not in deception and ignorance was thy greatest strength to be exercised. Thy triumph over the mind, unlike thy triumph over thy ancient foes, brings woe and desolation, without the ameliorating influence of right and justice.

Thy rule is that which paralyzes and blights human energy, and thy peace is the peace of death. Under thy sway the nations perish, and the clouds of blackness and despair lie, like a pall, upon the mind and conscience of the race. Should thy fell power again envelop humanity, without the light of philosophy to avert its effects, the human race might well imagine that thy ancient light of truth and reason had set in darkness forever.

CHAPTER IV.

THE INFLUENCE OF CHRISTIANITY UPON THE NATIONS OF WESTERN EUROPE AFTER THE DISINTEGRATION OF THE EMPIRE.

IT has often been asked by the defenders of Catholicism: What would have been the result had Julian lived long enough to have successfully inaugurated his policy as the governing principle of the Empire?

I will answer that question by saying, that my position at that period was a critical one, which, sometimes, marks an epoch in the world's history. I am not vain enough to ascribe to personal ability the results that might have followed; but I believe that had I succeeded in transferring the control of the youth of that period to the charge of philosophic minds, and held them there for one generation, the history of subsequent ages would have been for the better.

I meant to transfer the thought of my age *to other channels than those of military conquest, or servile obedience to imperial power.* It was a time in which the elements of a new nationality were germinating, and with discreet management there could have been a nationality born and developed which would have been free from the corruption and tyranny of Constantine and his successors, and also *free from the germs of a superstitious ecclesiasticism.* I had thought to elevate the old principles of religious toleration, and give protection to all faiths to such prominence *that never again would persecution for religion be permitted or desired by any subsequent ruler;* and I sought to do this by placing all religions upon a common footing before the civil law.

The determination of the Christian priesthood to monopolize the channels of learning, and their persistence in seeking to control the mental force of the Empire through their policy of confounding *the philosophic thought of the age with religious dogmas, inspired the thoughtful minds of my age with alarm,* lest the fundamental principles of truth and justice should be undermined, and the nation perish; and the unwise policy of persecution was at first attempted to crush out incipient danger to the State; but, like all mistaken measures of violence, proved to be a failure.

It has been said that, had I returned successfully from the campaigns against the Persians, I should have reinaugurated an era of persecution before which that of Diocletian would have been unworthy of mention; but that idea arose from the minds of those who were inflamed with that fanatical regard for religious ideas which carry men beyond the bounds of reason, or regard for truth.

I never believed in the policy which the former emperors adopted to crush out the incipient danger to the civil code; but I did believe that a policy of enlightenment of the ignorant concerning the foundation of all religions would lift the State above all danger from any faith.

I understood well the true source of the Christian ideas far better than most of their defenders; and had the policy I sought to reinstate been adopted by my successors, there would not have been retrogression of the mental progress in the provinces which composed the northern and western portions of the Empire.

These provinces were emerging from the barbaric plane to that position in the Empire where restraining force should have been of the military rather than of the ecclesiastical order; and the principles of obedience to the civil law, enforced upon all equally, would have effectually quelled the feudal spirit which supplanted the old policy.

Feudalism flourished in central Europe, because the priesthood were direct supporters of the principles of the supremacy of ecclesiastic law over the old Roman law of equality of individuals before the civil code.

While equality in Christ was preached to the people, *supremacy of the Church over the State was taught as the fundamental principle of the religion itself*, and no one who refused to accede to the demands of the earthly hierarchy could depend upon the support of that power for one instant in enforcing obedience to what remnant of civil authority remained.

It was a shrewd scheme upon the part of its devisers to obtain and retain power *for the sake of exercising power;* and they began at the fountain head of control by subordinating the intellectual faculties to the domination of the will. Hence, the first principle they adopted was that of unquestioning obedience to visible representation of invisible authority.

It was a perverted application of a great principle in philosophy, viz., obedience to truth as the true path of mental and moral perfection.

Christianity itself was the outcome of an effort to *harmonize the known truths of science with the fictions of previous generations;* but it never has been so understood by its devotees in mortal or spirit life. When it is understood, *the devotee ceases to be a Christian,* and becomes a scientist, or one who knows the true relations it holds in the department of ethics. If the moral elements which give it its real value were relegated to their true position, you would have Platonism of the purest type without the admixture of absurdities now supposed to be essential to the maintenance of social order, and which prevent the co-operation of all well-disposed minds upon earth in united action upon a plane of truth and purity. This has never been favored by the priesthood in Christian nations any more than among their predecessors, for, should the race once become enlightened sufficiently to understand the nature of life, *there will be no further necessity for the maintenance of a priestly order upon earth.*

There was a definite and positive influence continually exerted from this class of minds in the spirit world for several centuries succeeding the time of Diocletian and Galerius. Instead of forgiving their persecutors, as taught by their faith, they banded themselves to exert a direct influence upon the Empire itself, and determined upon its destruction. There were many among them who had suffered, and felt that the overthrow of the Empire would forever avert the possibility of further persecution; and so they joined hands with the crafty plotters, and really did more — through their influence in recalling to the minds of those upon earth their own sufferings — to change the feeling of the people against the national authority than any other force employed.

They did not understand the motive which led to their persecution, but they did understand that a government which made no discrimination between the crafty inciters of insurrection and the deluded victims was an evil to be removed; and the force of their mental opposition was felt on earth long after it was supposed to have passed away. It was directed mainly against the possibility of the civil power again being able to exert a persecuting policy against anyone for religious opinions; and let it be said in its behalf that never afterward was religious persecution practiced among the nations which succeeded the old Empire by the civil authorities, unless instigated by the religious elements of society who had obtained the supreme authority.

Of this latter class I propose to speak freely. When they had accomplished the overthrow of the civil authority, and substituted for its protecting influence the system of ecclesiastical supervision, *then began a chapter in the history of the race of a character that seems entirely anomalous.*

The intellect which should govern the will was subverted, and the very principles of law and order denied or prevented, and, if possible, obliterated from the mind.

Natural truth or natural phenomena was under the direct supervision of saints or devils, and no discovery in science allowed to be known which conflicted in the least degree with the established dogmas of the church. Men, elevated to high positions in the church, claimed to be the authoritative oracles or exponents of the Divine Mind by virtue of their office. It made no difference by what means they attained this position; the position conferred upon them the power and privilege to speak the will of Deity, and *give authoritative utterance to any falsehood as pure truth*. If experience had demonstrated the difference between truth and error to be defined and distinct, the dogma of the church pronouncing the error to be truth was held to be more binding upon the conscience than the demonstration of experience.

Under this policy craft and deception became prime factors in the development of the character of various nationalities, and treachery, with bloodshed, the normal condition of the race inhabiting Europe.

The result upon the people, subject to the varying strife, was incalculable both in the injury inflicted and the misery endured. The people sank under the weight of a tyranny unsupportable in its exactions, and hope of earthly redemption from the evils extant perished.

The priesthood indirectly encouraged the continuance of this policy by teaching the people that deliverance from the evils they endured *was only to be expected in the future life* as a reward for their faithful forbearance and endurance of the present, and never breathed a syllable of resistance to tyrannical authority, if that authority did not openly conflict with the principles inculcated by the priesthood.

It was a condition of transition in the mental realm, in which all concerned were verging from a chaotic mentality to a knowledge of the clear and well-defined relations which exist in the sphere of mental perfection.

I would not be unjust to the real value of the church in its attempt to control the barbarian elements, and its restraining power; but I do assert that it failed in educating the mentality of its devotees upon a basis of pure truth. It sought to govern by repression of the intellectual faculties, and held the race in darkness long after its mental eyes were formed to receive the influx of light.

It is here that its *power for evil is still exerted* upon the earth plane; for, although nature conceals the forming body at first in darkness, yet she does not always keep it there; and if perchance it does not come to a natural birth at the proper time, a monstrous and abnormal product results.

Christianity upon the earth plane is as unnatural and monstrous in its real nature as paganism was in the days of the later emperors. It is an overgrown combination of truth and error, and depends for its maintenance upon a continuation of belief in the errors which *craft fabricated to dominate the minds of the ignorant.* It does not differ materially from the errors of paganism which was taught in my age as truth; but there is this difference in effect: the errors of paganism were understood by the initiated, and taught to the enlightened in their true significance. They were not taught to the ignorant, and hence arose that mistaken policy, so prevalent wherever the Christian religion prevails, of *veiling the truth in mysterious symbols* which excite the imagination and foster gross superstitions.

Western Europe feels the incubus of this type of religion to this age, and has ever been the chief battle-ground between the forces marshaled under the banners of mental emancipation and those held in the bonds of superstition.

Those nations which have permitted the free expansion of intellectual power have made gigantic strides in the path of material as well as mental progress, while those that have been held by the dominant power at Rome are correspondingly weak and effeminate. The latter are unable to cope with the former upon any plane of action, and although often incited by the spirit hosts upon a similar plane of development to reinstate the old religious ideas in the superior nations by force, they lead their armies to disaster and ignominious failure.

To those upon the mortal plane this may seem to be a strange and doubtful solution of the problems involved in the political conditions of Europe; but I ask you to note this: ever since the religious revolution in Europe, by which papal authority was defied and denied by certain sections, liberty of conscience has been followed by the evolution of mental powers to that degree that religious superstition has had little effect in determining the political or mental status of the people, and the ablest minds have endeavored to shape the policy of the several governments upon the principles of equity and justice. This has given the people a chance to develop in all the lines which naturally make the individual or the nation powerful; and as nations are only aggregations of individuals, you see the result in the growth of governments that can meet and crush out the opposition of superstitious nations, no matter how powerful the latter may be in numbers or prestige.

It is the triumph of mind over matter, or the intellectual over the brutal elements in organization; and proportionally to freedom from the imposition of the will upon intellect does the nation advance in the path of true progress.

This progress is not entirely free from the influence of previous conditions of thought; but it has this in its favor: if the mind is partially subordinate to religious ideas, it is freed from the great error of regarding the ideas as having any visible authoritative representative upon earth, thus giving to the individual the right of private judgment, and calling into active exercise the faculties of judgment and discrimination. *He may worship the invisible God, but no longer does he bow to the visible representative;* and if he mistake not the influence emanating from decarnated spirits for the voice of Deity, he can develop the mental faculties without danger from any faith he may have in the protecting and inspiring relationship which his creed teaches him as existing between the Divine Mind and his own.

There is one danger that all religious persons are subject to in their ignorance of the natural relations existing between spirit and mortal life; and that danger consists in the *exercise of the will of deceptive minds through the law of mental magnetic induction.* It has been the great source of evils which have beset the civilized world for centuries, for it is only upon the mortal plane that its evils can be expressed in their full power. To the philosophic mind there is no desire to exercise power, save for the one motive of benefiting humanity. *To the religious mind there is a latent desire to govern for the sake of personal ambition*, and the Christian religion is no exception. It follows the autocratic system of gradation of office, and tries to introduce into the spheres of spiritual life the same principles which have generated the despotic dispositions upon earth. It has copied in this the intolerable customs of barbarian governments, and is *in direct conflict with the true ideas of republican institutions or republican principles.*

Europe, under the *régime* of the schools of Plato, would have been republican long ere this, for it had the germ principles of republicanism in its independence which the Roman arms never could subdue. Its outgrowth was seen in the flight of its best developed citizens to a strange country, where was implanted, as the basis of nationality, the old Roman idea of equality of all before the civil law, and the protection of all religions as of equal authority, but subordinate to the civil law, thus preventing the possibility of persecution by any.

This principle was as well known and understood by the philosophic minds of my age as by the founders of the great modern Republic, and it was my intention, had I lived, to have held the Empire upon this line of development; for, with the most intelligent men as counselors, the civil authority would not have transcended its legitimate functions, and the people have become imbued with a love instead of dread of it. They would not have turned to the priesthood as the true exponents of human rights, and, in time, the superstitions of the past would have faded away from their minds as realities, as they have from your own.

It is unnecessary for me to designate the individual states which have been the chief exponents of the principles I have mentioned; but it is enough to affirm that those which have abrogated entirely the claims of Romish ecclesiastical control have flourished, and are the strong powers of modern civilization, while those which have held, and still hold, to the Catholic superstitions of the past are proportionally weak and disintegrated in the elements which generate a strong nationality.

CHAPTER V.

THE RISE OF RATIONALISM IN MODERN EUROPE, AND ITS RELATIONS TO CIVILIZATION.

I AM requested to write a chapter upon the secret sources of that peculiar phase of modern thought which has been expressed by a type of mind generated in the schools of science and philosophy, and which is termed rationalism.

This subject necessarily involves much that to mortal vision is strange and incomprehensible, because it is not confined to special schools of thought, but is as liable to be found among isolated thinkers as among the most learned professors of the various departments of science and philosophical research. In fact, it is more often found in greater perfection among the isolated thinkers than in any of the schools; for, properly, the power of generation is different from distribution; and the power of generation of ideas does not differ in essence from the same principle in organic or formative construction.

Rationalism is the outcome of the cultivation of the perception and study of phenomena. It holds the relation to science that experiment in science has to obtaining an accurate knowledge of phenomena. It may be said to be the highest form of intellectual evolution, because the intellectual powers are the only factors employed in forming deductions from the phenomena.

Belief has no part in the field of rationality, or, at least, no part in the premises upon which the deductions are formed; and the only function that belief has in a rational mind is to incite that mind to the process of experiment to determine the truth about any subject.

Rationalism, then, may be said to be the natural result of a combined relation of science and philosophy, while a combination of ignorance and dissimulation produces the varied forms of superstitions which, under the name of religion, has sought to subject the mental powers to its sway.

In the days of the later Cæsars, the great contest between rationalistic thought and superstitious belief was waged between the schools of Alexandria and the priests of Rome. It is not generally known upon earth, at this day, what was really taught in these schools; but if you will once understand that a great nation cannot exist without its schools of a medical and legal character, you can readily understand their nature.

The schools were the *foci* of the intellectual life of the Empire. The physicians and lawyers, the army and naval cadets (as you would call them) the candidates for civil and judicial offices,— all received their first impressions of their life work from the various schools scattered throughout the Empire; but the chief seats of the educational force in the

Empire were at Athens and Alexandria. These cities held the reins of formative power; for, as they furnished the controlling ideas to the youth of the Empire, the Empire was more subject to them, in many respects, than to its armies.

I am more anxious that the world should understand the influence of these schools upon the mental state of my age than that the mere victories of the Roman arms should be held in such high estimation, for as long as the intellectual life of the nation was cherished, so long did the Empire flourish; and it was only when they were suppressed that disintegration and anarchy supervened.

These schools of Grecian science and Alexandrian literature were rationalistic in their influence upon the intellectual and moral relations of the youth. Because of this the religious element feared them, and plotted their destruction. The religious element in the Empire was not ignorant of scientific truth. It knew the baseless character of the gods, or, rather, it knew their true character; but *it was not honest in its dealings with the populace*, and it lost the confidence of the enlightened classes who would have suffered it to perish from neglect had not the boldest scheme ever devised by priestcraft been concocted and inaugurated at Rome to preserve the power, while it changed the external form.

This scheme has but recently been brought to mortal knowledge, but it has been known in spirit life for centuries, and the work of Strauss,* in Germany, was one effort to give to mortals a hint of the

* David Strauss, a renowned German writer on the Christian religion.

true source of the present religious belief of modern
Europe.

Other minds have caught glimpses of the truth,
but so dense was the darkness, and so doubtful the
proof, that they have hardly dared give to the world
the true idea of the modern subject of religious
worship.

I saw clearly in my earth life that the Christian
Deity was not better in his nature than the old
deities of Rome and Greece; and as they only represented ideal conditions of human development, I
rather encouraged than discouraged their worship by
that class of minds who must have a visible embodiment of principles.

But I never worshiped them in such a sense as the
Christian priesthood have asserted; for when once
the mind has risen to the plane of a rational understanding of religious belief, *it no longer can be held
in the bonds of any creed*, however that creed may
seem to embody divine wisdom.

When the conflict between the schools of rational
thought and the ideas of priestly subservience arose,
the former sought no weapons save those of reason
and truth. Not so the latter. They catered to
the dominant weaknesses of the reigning emperors,
and sought through their superstitions to supplant
the old ideas of philosophy by force; and with the
strong arm of the civil law they closed the doors
whereby intellectual discovery could have a chance
of expression, and for a thousand years held those
doors closed against the ingress and egress of thought
which threatened in any degree the overthrow of

their supremacy. Nor did their work end here. They first sought alliance with the civil power; and, after this was obtained, they brought to bear the influence of direct control over its functions, and then the exercise of its functions, to prevent any change in human thought upon the earth plane. Any change they pronounced to be worthy of malediction and condemnation.

Under such conditions no wonder the provinces of Europe, which were emerging from a barbaric to a civilized condition, relapsed into a condition worse than their first estate, and for centuries remained in a state of savagery that seemed to preclude any hope of elevation.

I am no optimist in my estimate of the relationship which error holds in its power of depriving individuals or nations of their natural birthright; and when I have seen the myriad hosts of these provinces engaged in battle array for no aim worthy of bloodshed, with no well-defined object whereby either party would gain any end worthy of strife, I have contrasted these wars, which have deluged the plains of Europe with blood and rapine, with the wars of the Empire, which always were waged against the principle of disintegration and in behalf of a national unity of purpose. When our arms were successful, we threw the protection of the civil law over the conquered, and they became integral parts of the nation; but the wars which have devastated modern Europe have left the various participants with no other results than their mutual exhaustion and ina-

bility to inflict further misery upon their citizens
for a season.

The spirit of peace and fraternity is not authoritative when standing armies are maintained at such
a cost to the productive energy of a country; and I
feel justified in asserting that the military spirit, cul-
tivated by ancient Rome, was superior in its motives
to that which supplanted it in Christian Europe.

There is no hope of progressive development as
long as the military force of a nation is subservient
to the religious instead of the civil power; and before there could be a return to the principles which
made Roman authority in the age of the Cæsars so
effective in behalf of intellectual culture and mental
illumination, the religious force had to be broken,
which was accomplished by two great agencies, viz..
the art of printing, and the religious revolt of the
sixteenth century.

The art of printing was the opening wedge in the
solid phalanx of superstition which had enveloped
the mentality of Europe; for it gave Grecian literature a chance to be recognized in its true relation to
modern literary culture; and the students in the
universities found that there had been ideas recorded
which betokened a type of mental growth equal in
intellectual power, if not in religious zeal, to more
recent instructors of the youth. The use of the
types gave religion an inspection not foreseen by the
inventor, for it brought the two systems in direct
contrast; and although the superstitions of the pagan deities were relegated to the realm of mythology,

their counterparts in Christianity began to be questioned by enlightened and thoughtful minds.

The first fruits of this questioning were directed toward the basis of ecclesiastical authority, and upon the discovery *that this emanated from the pontifical dictator of Rome,* the northern sections of Europe revolted in a body, but did not emerge fully into the position of religious independence. It was a partial victory for rationalism, for the reason was appealed to against the authority of tradition; but the devotees of authority were in excess of the devotees of reason, so that the allegiance to papal authority was transferred to the purported divinely inspired *dictum* of a written volume.

It was like all great movements in mental revolutions; a compromise of forces whereby the mind is impelled in a circle instead of a straight line, and the mentality of a large portion of the revolted provinces *circulates around the central ideas of the religion* which it refuses to recognize from its arbitrary claims to their allegiance.

Here we have a chance for rational thought, but not a free field for its full expression; for the mind which transfers its allegiance from one exponent to another of the same central thought *cannot analyze the central thought in an unbiased manner,* and hence cannot form a reliable conclusion as to its true value.

This is the trouble with all minds which are only partial rationalists in dealing with the religious questions of this age. *They confine their thoughts to the external expression of the religion* rather than upon the internal relations of religion to natural principles, and become bewildered in their conclusions respecting it. They can perceive the absurdity of worshiping Jupiter or Diana, who once stood for the creative power and virgin purity, but they do not see that the idea of creative power uniting with virgin purity to produce a perfect type of manhood is *only another form of the idea* which pagan Rome taught for centuries before the Christian era.

They worship the visible embodiment of these *principles and results under other names indeed*, but if the claim of primal authority belongs to any religion, it belongs to the originator of the idea rather than to the recipient of it.

Almost the first result of the modern intellectual awaking in Europe was the comparing and contrasting of ideas concerning primitive religions; and the outcome of that work is seen in the growth of rationalism in place of theology in all civilized and enlightened communities. In sympathy with this elevation of thought, I should add, is the direct influence of the hosts of intelligences, unseen to mortal vision, who direct their powers of thought upon the organisms upon earth best fitted to express advanced ideas.

Earthly recipients of this wisdom are marked examples of the power of rationalistic thought, and prominent exponents of the ideas which *propel* the human race upon the earth plane *upon* the path of science and discovery as the true methods of ascertaining truth.

To them *no religious idea is sacred from analysis*, and to them comes silently the aid of minds who have long since emerged from the realm of mysticism to the pure light of unadulterated truth. They cannot be blind, if they would, and they would not conceal from the ignorant and erring upon earth the true relations of all souls to eternal principles and everlasting results. To them the world will owe its redemption from ignorance and error, and to them, also, too often has the martyr's crown been given.

CHAPTER VI.

THE CAUSE OF THE ANTAGONISM BETWEEN RATIONALISM AND ALL RELIGIOUS SYSTEMS OF THE PRESENT AGE BASED UPON CHRISTIANITY.

IT is necessary that I write specifically upon the minor relations of religious systems in order to explain the antagonism which has ever been existent between philosophy and all types of Christianity since its advent upon the earth plane.

In order to do this, I must first explain the origin of polytheism, and its relations to mental development in mortal life. It seems puzzling to you that men ever could believe in a multiplicity of gods, and that religious systems differed so much in various parts of the Empire. But if you once can understand what we meant by the term gods, you will see that Grecian polytheism was not any more superstitious in its dogmas than the Christian polytheism which succeeded it.

Gods or deities meant, in our times, the creating and preserving force which pervaded all phenomena. We saw the phenomena of nature arising and advancing from an unknown and invisible source, and that source we called Deity, or Divine Wisdom.

We applied this term because it was so different from human wisdom which could only create other forms, or manipulate matter after it had been formed, and because there were manifestations of human intelligences from the invisible world, we connected them with the first ideal, but as subordinate exhibitions of Divine Wisdom.

To the primitive creative power was attributed the function of supreme control over all others, under the title of (Greek) Zeus; (Roman) Jupiter; (Hebrew) Jehovah; (Egyptian) Osiris, etc. These words expressed essentially the same idea to the worshipers of each nation, and were interchangeable in the translation of language.

The exhibition of spirit intelligences under the titles of angels, demons, spirits, etc., was regarded by us as the work of lesser gods or deities, who were invoked as the special guardians of places or individuals. Really, they were the spirits of people who had left the earth life, but were attracted to those still there from various motives. They were in all grades of mental and moral development, and expressed all the attributes of the grades to which they belonged. Hence, they were observed to be affected with human passions, and exhibited the follies and frailties which betokened a mortal origin. Some of them were crafty and ambitious to exercise power over those still in mortal life; and, by skillfully concealing from their earthly mouthpieces their real nature, expressed through them their commands, giving rise to the belief that, in so doing, they were voicing the will of the Supreme Intelligence.

It was by this method of spiritual instruction that the great differences which arose among the polytheists can be explained; for the oracles which were consulted, and believed to be the voice of the Supreme Power, often were nothing more than deceptive spirits who sought in this manner to palm off upon the ignorant mortal their own opinions as the decrees of the Almighty; and, as there were different oracles, there were many revelations which were contradictory in statements, and absurd in their meaning.

There were some shrines which were devoted to the discovery and propagation of truth; and, if the seeker at such fountain was pure in motive, he generally obtained a truthful answer to his questions.

It was this mixture of error and truth at the various centers of spiritual intercourse that created the diversity and antagonism between the religious ideas in the ancient world, and, especially, between the pagan and Christian believers in my age.

The philosophers understood the general principles of spiritual intercourse, or, at least, they knew that a large share of the so-called revelations of the oracles were either the fabrications of the priesthood or the works of a class of mischievous spirits which infested the temples, inciting their dupes to evil.

The purest type of philosophy did not teach that the Divine Mind had ever been embodied, although Plato had expressed the idea of it in some of his teachings, meaning by it that the perfect type of manhood was like the highest expression of Deific wisdom.

It was this idea that the Christian priesthood

taught as having been realized in their founder, and in order to insure his acceptance with that class of minds who still believed in re-incarnation of the soul, they claimed for their deity a double nature, or that of a Divine man.

There was nothing essentially new in this claim, for the Greek and Roman theology taught that Divinity could be, and often was, incarnated in the great and striking types of manhood who were apotheosized after death; but the Christians claimed a monopoly of the idea, and, while they denied its possibility to others, based their own hope of eternal happiness upon the truth, as they supposed, of only one Divine incarnation ever having occurred upon earth.

The absurdity of this claim was so apparent to the intelligent minds of my age that we hardly cared to attempt to seriously refute it, and so, by default, the antidote for the error was omitted until the earth was poisoned by it, and the mental powers of the race were impaired almost beyond recovery.

It is thus that systems replete with error arise and become intrenched in the affections, and lead the minds of their devotees away from the truth in its purity. *Christianity holds in its principles many, if not all, of the essential features of pagan mythology and pagan philosophy.* It has no more intrinsic worth than the systems it has supplanted, but it should be better understood in its true relations to those systems. It was the realization of an effort to produce uniformity of religious worship throughout the Em-

pire, and its success was commensurate with its incorporation of the essential features of other religions.

It is useless to talk of Christianity in its primitive
purity, for it never had a primitive condition in which
it could be free from connection with ideas *that were
in existence long ere the term Christian was known.*

It is not essential that I write of the primitive
worship of ancient Rome, or of the nations composing
the Empire, but rather to illuminate the obscurity
which surrounds the nativity of the Christian ideas
that have descended to this age.   These ideas were
mainly the offspring of two types of mental development, viz., the purest maxims of philosophy and the
allegorical fictions of the priesthood.   Their combination, in the form of Christianity, was a mistaken
policy upon the part of the originators, inasmuch as,
with the new form of expression, there was a *repression of the knowledge of its true source.*

The fiction of deific intercourse with the women
of earth was preserved in the fabulous account of the
miraculous conception and birth of Jesus from a virgin mother.   *The idea was not new, but it was sur-
rounded with a halo of sanctity as the only case that
ever really occurred upon earth.*   It was a familiar
idea to most of the primitive converts, but it was
also taught that it was a finality, and never could
occur again.   It was so with most of the doctrines
which constituted the body of divinity among the
various sects of the Christians throughout the Empire.

The ideas were taken from the old religions, but
changed enough to appear to be new to the ignorant

multitude who adopted them. The **philosophers** looked on in amazement at the obtuseness of the believers in the new religion *who could not discern the identity of the old legends under their new phraseology;* but the interested propagators of the **ideas** seemed smitten with a fanaticism **akin** to madness, and never **ceased their efforts to supplant the old** divinities **with the** new, although **the latter was** no more worthy of homage than the others.

There seemed to be a determination upon the part of many otherwise intelligent minds *to make the religious nature the chief object of cultivation,* and thereby bring the race upon a plane of development which should preclude any danger to its eternal welfare. I can account for it only upon the basis of a desire of the crafty to govern through superstition, and the dupes to ensure their **own personal safety in** the world **of** spirits.

The doctrine **of immortality was generally accepted** and understood **by the pagan religionists, and the** phenomena of a spiritual nature were observed and studied by the philosophical minds of all ages; but there were **not** well defined or well expressed ideas concerning its nature and laws, and herein, I think, the Christian priesthood exercised their **greatest** power, for they purported **to understand and appor**tion to humanity a **certain knowledge of the princi**ples governing the eternal world.

They assumed **to be** *the only guardians of this knowledge, and the only authorized channels for its dispensation upon the earth,* and by their very assumption gained credence from the ignorant, which **they** have

held since by adopting the policy of maintaining
their position through *the cultivation of ignorance as
necessary to belief.*

The philosophic mind in my age, and in all ages,
has never claimed absolute knowledge of truth in
any department as a finality; but while accepting
the truth, where known, has rather made *it a basis
for the increase of knowledge,* and especially in that
department of spiritual science which had, at best,
been but partially explored, did it dare to pronounce
its decree save in the most guarded manner.

*It knew enough of the principles of immortal ex-
istence* to regard them as factors which must not be
overlooked in estimating the value of mortal life;
but there never was that disposition to dogmatize
about the conditions which has characterized the
Christian mind ever since Christianity has become
the recognized exponent of a future existence.

There were too many problems involved in the
subject of immortal life for anyone to assume authority to dogmatize about, and it has been left to the
champions of Christianity in the mortal realm to
definitely set boundaries upon the eternal destiny of
the soul, and to maintain that their dogmas have the
sanction and decree of the Divine Mind.

This assumption lies at the basis of the antagonism between Rationalism and Christianity. It existed in my age, and ever since has disturbed the
relations existing between minds imbued *with a love
of pure truth, and those content with accepting the
imperfect knowledge of a partial exposition of truth.*
There seems to be no middle ground for a compro-

mise of ideas as long as the Christian world reso-
lutely maintains its present position towards honest
doubters of its claims to infallibility.

The reluctance of the clerical or ecclesiastical
mind *to concede a possibility of error* in the foundation of their religious system compels the rationalists
to conclude that the religious world is stranded upon
a myth, and is in as helpless a condition at this age
as at any period in the world's history.

The error is so inwoven in the life essence of a
portion of the race that it seems impossible to attack
it without serious injury to *the truth veiled under
the myth*, and thoughtful minds shrink from assailing
what really is a great obstacle to the successful progress of the race.

Some daring hands are raised in protest against
the imposition of falsehood as truth; but, as yet,
their work is but partially understood, and the crafty
defenders of religious mythology in this age hold
almost indisputable power over large numbers who
imagine their future eternal welfare depends upon
their ignorance of any ideas except those pertaining
to established religious dogmatism.

The rationalist, however, has this in his favor: *he
is able to wait*, and only needs to have the true ideas
advanced in an intelligible manner to ensure a consideration by those minds that are naturally progressive, and by the aid of the spirit hosts, who are in
sympathy with liberal thought, *a rational conception
of spiritualistic thought can be given and understood
by intelligent minds upon the earth plane.*

I say *intelligent* minds; for the superstitious devotees of any creed are not intelligent in their advocacy of their peculiar dogmas. They lack the fundamental principles of **spiritual** perception, *and cannot become* **versed** *in spiritual* **truth** **until** *that faculty is awakened.*

Even the rationalist, who lacks this power of spiritual insight, will be deficient in this essential point; and, if not careful, will make as great a mistake as does his Christian opponent in his estimate of the true relations of earthly life to the spiritual world. He can remedy his deficiency, however; and, if he exerts his powers of discrimination whereby truth is judged by reason, will be far more likely to become spiritually enlightened than his blind opponent whose mental powers are developed under the influence of a system of positive error which has been mistaken for so many centuries as the only true source of spiritual light and knowledge.

CHAPTER VII.

THE SPIRITUAL MOVEMENT OF THE PRESENT AGE, AND ITS RELATION TO THE CONFLICT BETWEEN RATIONALISM AND RELIGIOUS TRADITION.

In observing the changes incident to the mortal conditions of the race, I have often witnessed the astonishment which the historians of earth express at the sudden revolutionary transitions which mark the epochs of history. It is said by some of them that, in order to obtain a correct idea of ancient civilization, one must abandon the idea that the ancient peoples, whose civil and moral code has been transmitted to posterity as the greatest exhibition of divine wisdom, were not alike in thought or feeling to the generations of the present age.

There is a general feeling on earth that, in some mysterious manner, the inhabitants of the world, two or three thousand years ago, were so different that the residents of the eternal world could come in close relationship to favored mortals, and express the will and commands of the Supreme Creator.

This idea has been diligently fostered by the religious teachers of the present age, and upon it is founded the systems of religious dogmas in different nations. The practical effect of belief in this idea is to prevent the present generation on earth from the consideration of its truth or falsity, and substitute for it the principle of acceptance without question, because it has been taught and believed for so many centuries to be the truth.

I have written about the nature of ancient pagan worship, but I shall have to state here a fact about the Hebrew nation that is not generally known. It sought to preserve and hold intact the monotheism of Egypt, and was really the pioneer of the present age in preserving the original philosophy of the ancient world from priestly corruption.

There was one weak point in the Hebraistic theology. The controlling mind from the spirit realm, who announced himself as the guardian power of that nation, was unfortunate in giving it the impression that he was the Eternal Being. He was not wholly responsible for this idea becoming so firmly implanted in that nation, for his motive was to prevent, if possible, the nation from lapsing into the barbaric licentiousness of the surrounding nations; but the priesthood that he instituted represented to the people that this deity was the Great I Am.

I have conversed with many spirits who lived at the time the Hebrew code was adopted, and their testimony is invariably this: that it was very much altered after the conquest of Jerusalem by the Assyrians, but that originally the spirit guardian only sought to have a nation that should preserve the idea intact of one controlling power in the universe;

but, unfortunately for the world, he was misrepresented as claiming to be that power.

You can see by this that no matter how true and pure a spirit may be in motive, if he delegates to mortals authority, in any degree, to represent his ideas, he will always be at the disadvantage of misrepresentation on earth, if his reputed agents choose to have it so.

The practical outcome of this effort was the institution of a priesthood in behalf of monotheism, but, nevertheless, a priesthood which, like all priesthoods, was as liable to become corrupt and unreliable as that which existed in the polytheistic nations.

I do not mean to be unjust toward individual members of the various priestly orders which have from age to age ministered at the altars of the various religions. I know the difficulties which a false position ever entails upon any class of men in the mortal or even spiritual sphere of life; but I must say here that the trouble which afflicts religions of all kinds is this: no one in mortal life ever could truthfully claim that he or she voiced the will of the Eternal Being, and all statements that they did were impositions, if from the spirit world, or fabrications, if from the mortal world.

This brings me directly to a consideration of the oracular utterances of all deities. There are certain natural relations existing between organisms in mortal and spiritual life whereby the mental power, or thought of each, can be transmitted. This method is essentially the same in all nations, and the ideas given through it correspond with the grades of mental development of the operator upon the spirit side, modified somewhat in expression by the mental development of the medium upon the earth side. The natural result of the use of this power is the transmission of some ideas which may or may not be exact truths about the subject under consideration, proportionally to the knowledge and honesty of the spiritual transmitter.

When any mind claims to know more than it has obtained by knowledge from study, observation, and development, it is a clear case of egotistical assertion, if not positive falsehood; and when revelations, purporting to come from the spiritual world, give statements which transcend the ability of a spiritual mentality to attain, they may safely be rejected as false from the foundation.

This is the trouble with all religious systems that have a basis upon the claims of a divine and final revelation.

NO SUCH REVELATION HAS EVER BEEN, OR CAN, BE GIVEN TO MAN,

as long as the race exists under its present conditions.

Even granting the existence of a Supreme Mind, it becomes evident that no mind upon the lower plane is, or can be, of a caliber sufficient to fully express its thought, and that fact alone bars the world from receiving a complete revelation of its will and purposes. All that purport to be such bear in their own assertions the evidence of their fictitious character, and are only found in any age of the world

among the ignorant and superstitious minds who
readily fall a prey to the designs of craft and ambition.

*The deity of any people generally reflects the dis-
tinctive traits of character which the mental and moral
grade of that people generate*, and, consequently, the
God of any nation is a type of the national character,
as expressed through its priesthood.

There should be some explanation given about the
ideas now believed concerning the Divine Character
and those held by the ancient world. The latter
expressed their religious differences through the worship of different deities, each deity being a distinct
expression of some central idea; while in your age
these differences are expressed through different sects
who regard the Supreme Divinity as embodied in the
special ideas around which center their peculiar sect.

Hence arise the most diverse forms of thought and
expression concerning the nature of the Deity, often
so contradictory that intelligent minds upon the earth
plane conclude that the whole subject of religion and
religious worship is based upon the fabulous and vis-
ionary speculation of ill-balanced minds of all ages,
who have sought to bind the world with mental
chains which should never be broken.

In their iconoclastic zeal to break these chains,
they have overlooked the one great truth underlying
all religious systems which, once understood, enables
the mind to dispense with them as finalities, and
relegate them to their proper position in the world's
history.

This is nothing more than *the natural relationship*

which exists, and ever has existed between the physical and spiritual conditions of life. It is the only
idea that has never been completely extinguished in
the dark clouds of superstition which have settled
like a pall upon the lands under the immediate sway
of the Christian and Mohammedan religions.

It will be received by faith, however, rather than
by sight, and be vague and unsatisfactory to some,
while to others it will seem to be sure and conclu-
sive. The former will not understand the reason of
their doubts, nor the latter the true ground of their
faith, until they are instructed as to the nature of
this spiritual influx which, at times, permeates the
moral and mental atmosphere of earth.

I would like to say to those of earth, once for all,
that no spiritual movement upon the earth plane ever
exists *which does not have its inception in the world
of souls*, whose residents, by availing themselves of
the natural relations existing between the two realms,
can affect their earth brethren. When the source of
the influx is from a high moral and philosophical grade
of spirits, you have a revival of the arts and sciences ;
while, on the other hand, if of a lower type, you have
a revival of obsolete religious ideas, backed by seem-
ingly an invincible power of will which convinces
the most hardened and degraded souls that there exists a spiritual force which is able to compel attention, if not to enforce obedience ; and, by appeals to
the fears, often induces a partial change of conduct.
This is the distinctive type of thought generated by
religious spirits, and is *the power depended upon,
under the title Holy Spirit*, to produce the peculiar

mental phenomena upon the earth plane known as religious revivals.

Their benefit, when conducted by spirit forces which seek to improve the moral condition of men, might seem to more than counterbalance their evil effects; but, like all systems of mingled truth and error, the evil resulting from such excitements often exceeds the good to such a degree as to cause thoughtful minds to seriously consider the advisability of longer countenancing them as necessary or reformatory.

The failure to command the respect and confidence of thoughtful minds is their great weakness. *They do not have the support and approval of the wisest* in the world of spirits, because they know that no system of religion or morals which does not incorporate the motive power of the whole truth, and its revealment, is a safe system for spirits or mortals to adopt. This, the present religious systems of earth, do not do any more than those of twenty centuries ago. *The pagan priesthood concealed the truth, and falsified at will,* where they considered it expedient; and the Christian priesthood cannot, in truth, claim to have been much better. *They have arrayed themselves against the advent of spiritual truth through the only channels whereby it can reach the earth, with explanations of its nature,* and consequently their temples are void of spiritual power of a truthful character. *They abound with the ignorant and undeveloped spirits of all classes and conditions who act upon* and through sensitives who worship there in such a manner as to cause the thoughtful and considerate to wonder if the heavenly mansions are any more likely to abound in moral and mental excellence than if the old deities of Rome had never been supplanted by the modern conceptions of the Divine nature.

Religious spirits are chiefly remarkable for the extreme solicitude which they manifest *lest the moral status of the world should deteriorate if the religious element* should fail to retain control of the educational interests of the race. They cling with pertinacity to the idea of the extreme sanctity of religious dogmas, and imbue their recipients on earth with similar ideas, thus preserving from age to age the confidence in the necessity of a religious education to preserve the world from moral corruption.

Through their earth channels, they *convey false ideas relative to the true status of a spiritual life,* and prevent the influx, as far as possible, of truthful statements which might be of great benefit to minds upon earth. It is the part of charity to suppose this is done with pure motives upon the part of many, but truth compels me to assert that *no spirit can use this natural power for influencing mortals without becoming instructed as to its true nature;* and then, if it fails to convey truthful ideas to the earthly recipient, the spirit becomes a participant in spiritual deception, and consequent self-degradation.

Because of the determined opposition upon the part of these spirits to the spread of spiritual truths on earth, there has arisen a powerful combination in the spiritual world of those who have knowledge and a love of the truth in its purity *to reach the earth with ideas of a truthful character concerning the relations*

*of mortal and spirit life; but these spirits stand aloof
from any connection with the religious systems, save
as explanatory expositors of them.*

They are rationalists in theory, and scientists in
practice, founding their deductions upon the most
careful experiments in the realm of material and
spiritual forces; and their ideas when received and
understood *instruct the minds upon earth upon the
only solid basis of spiritual intelligence in either
world.*

They have watched the race for centuries, touch-
ing a brain here and there with the sacred impulse
of living truth, irrespective of religious dogmas, and,
when possible, lifting the veil for a season from those
minds whose natural growth tends to lift them above
the domination of error. Religion has made martyrs
to truth in some ages, but the world has been impelled
forward sufficiently to now protect its scientific teachers from religious persecution; and, at this age, one
mind — like a Darwin, or Tyndall, or Huxley — is
worth more to the race than all the popes or prelates
that have ever existed, for the former have taught
upon the earth plane *the preliminary ideas of advanced minds in the world of spirits.*

These ideas, supplemented by the facts of a truthful spiritual phenomena, will give the world the true
revelation of the spiritual nature, and, when expressed
in intelligible language, will not fail to educate and
instruct all that come under their influence.

It will be the redeeming force, and, I might truthfully affirm, the only redeeming force that can change
the present irrational and oppressive policy that

religion, through its various types and agencies, has entailed upon the race.

There is no necessity for concealment or craft by this class of instructors, and those upon the earth plane who receive them will connect themselves with the elevated and enlightened minds of past ages, who will freely instruct them in those departments which their natural talents best adapt them to pursue while in the earth life, and insure their happiness and welfare in the life eternal.

CHAPTER VIII.

THE RESULT OF THE EFFORTS OF ADVANCED SPIRITS TO INSTRUCT THE PEOPLE OF EARTH IN THE PRINCIPLES OF SPIRITUAL SCIENCE.

THE reader, by this time, may have discerned that there is a direct connection between the mental growth of man in the earth sphere and the spirit hosts who have gradually been transplanted from that condition to another life, if I have told the truth about the immortal life.

I am aware of the imperfect expression of my thoughts through this method, but the principles which I imbibed under the instruction of Maximus have ever been a guiding power in my spiritual existence; and, in obedience to those instructions, I feel inclined to write one more chapter upon the consequences which may result when a knowledge of the true principles of spirituality shall be understood upon the earth.

I know full well *the determined hostility of the dominant spiritual force, acting in behalf of religion* upon the earth plane, to prevent a knowledge of spiritual truth in its purity from reaching mortals;

but, as the mists of the morning are dispelled by the
rising of the sun in his brilliant radiance, so will the
mists of error, now brooding over the minds of men,
be lifted by the rising of the true light of spiritual
knowledge.   This light is the emancipating power
which acts most effectually when it compels the mental powers of the race to recognize the presence of a
force acting upon the intellectual nature. The recipient begins an incipient questioning of the ideas that
he has hitherto held by faith.   He cannot help the
doubt which may arise, although he may seek to
stifle it as wrong and dangerous.

The very fact that he doubts *is the strongest proof
of intellectual activity;* for doubt precedes thought
as much as belief tends to prevent thought, and produce credulity. No mind, under the influence of
active thought, can fail to feel the effect, and those
individuals are ever the most progressive who wel-
come the expression of all grades of thought, in order
that the truth of each grade may become the basis of
a true estimate in forming conclusions.

The greatest obstacle upon the earth plane *is the
unwillingness of certain minds to admit the possibility
of a false basis* upon which their conclusions were
deduced, and the consequent errors which have
clouded the mental horizon of the race.

When I revert to the knowledge of the past ages,
as exhibited by the types of human development in
Greece and Egypt, I am astounded, or should be, did
I not know the reasons why intelligent minds of
this age should suppose that humanity could produce
such specimens of intellectual grandeur in the condi-

tions which are now taught to moderns as having
existed then. "Is it possible to grow grapes of thorns
and figs of thistles" in the mental and moral realm?
Would the ancient world ever have arisen to its
hights of civilization upon a different basis than that
existent today? No! The principles of nature are
eternal; the results are the same in all ages where
causative power is the same, and in your highest
types of intellectual and moral supremacy you have
the same examples that the world has had in all
ages.

When the individual absorbed the principles in his
own character *he radiated them to the world, without
blemish or defect.* Where he failed to do this, he was
only a mouthpiece for the invisible intelligence who
sought to inculcate the idea, even if at the risk
of misconception and misconstruction; and the dis-
seminator of the idea, on the mortal side, never was
regarded in the world of spirits as more than a mirror
for the reflection of another's mental acquirements.

The methods whereby the ideas are given to the
race upon the earth are not so essential to be understood by mortals as to be utilized for them; but
they are not mysteries to those of us who have *the
knowledge of the forces of the spiritual realm.* We
center the forces of any special line of thought upon
some sensitive brain in the earth life who reflects the
ideas to his fellow-mortals in the form of written or
spoken language.

The direct recipient of the forces might not understand the true sources of his inspiration, and if of a
well-developed brain might be justified in supposing

that he was the generator of the ideas. He might never know of a spiritual existence in its true relations to earthly life, and yet reflect the ideas of some of its inhabitants in a state of great perfection. These ideas would generally be best expressed in the particular department of thought that his own brain had been developed to transmit from the mind; still, he would be reflecting to a great degree the thought that had been impressed upon him by the direct action of the external force, but in harmony with it, and the idea would reach the earth as a new impelling force in behalf of truth.

This is the general method used by advanced spirits to bring their ideas before men upon the earth plane. They are not ambitious to be recognized as advanced by the minds of mortals, nor to stimulate the defective traits of character in many of the earthly mouthpieces, by giving them any knowledge of their true character, hence they may be appropriately denominated the *silent force which works rather than talks in the world's history, shaping the current of events* so that the race shall make some progress from generation to generation in spite of all the short-sighted opposition from that grade of thought expressed by the less enlightened. Their work is in accord with the *principles of Nature as expressed through evolution;* and they do not wish a forced and unnatual growth of man in any department of his character. But one thing they do wish, and will make ample provision to effect, viz., the utmost liberty of the individual to develop his spiritual nature under the knowledge of truth in its purity; and this

is why the world is continually receiving an influx
of ideas, all tending to axalt the natural rights of
the individual, as of greater consequence than any
privilege of special classes.

Hence, the social and political upheavings which
have marked the progress of the race have tended to
bring the individual more and more into prominence
as the great factor in the problem; and, while one
political system after another is tried and laid aside,
those only are secure which command the good will
and voluntary support of the individual.

To the advanced spirit, in his estimate of the outcome of personal existence, *all souls are of equal
value.*

There are none so poor and obscure as to be unworthy of notice; and none so low and degraded as
to be hopeless of redemption. There is no disposition to separate the good and bad as individuals, but
a determination that those who have unfortunately
been deprived of the chance for a good development
in the earth life *shall have a chance to outgrow* the
evil results of that misfortune. Their ideas, when
expressed through earthly channels, may seem vision-
ary and utopian, but they know, as no mortal can
know, the secret causes of the results known on
earth as good and evil. They can give to mortals
the true solution of the great mystery; but, at present, they are more interested in bringing about such
conditions that the race may become self-instruct-
ive rather than dependent upon the ideas of others.
The work of this class of minds is seen and felt in its
best results in all departments of material science

that betoken advanced civilization. There is scarcely a discovery or invention perfected upon the earth plane of any great importance that does not have its real author from among the unseen but ever-powerful and active body of silent workers. They perfect its powers ere a knowledge of its details are impressed upon some sensitive brain upon earth; but in time the world has it, and reaps the benefit of it, even if its true progenitor is never known there.

It is not essential that the personal name or fame of the true inventor or discoverer should be known, but that the power of the idea should be embodied in form, so that the race may receive an impetus by it to other attainments.

The world moves upward in this way, and the race improves under the stimulus of embodied ideas; but the end sought by the spirit world, represented by this type, is not acquisition of material wealth for the few, but the fullest development of the intellectual and moral powers of all who share in the beneficial results of their labors.

The stimulus to endeavor through these channels is as powerful upon the peasant as the prince; and the great changes which now mark the epochs in the world's history are brought out more often by the sons of toil than the offspring of luxury. It is a significant rebuke to the world in its estimate of the value of rank or position that the deeds of the greatest importance to the world's progress are wrought by the hands and brain of the apparently obscure and insignificant; and the old idea, that royal blood and nobility of rank are necessary factors to success, is entirely ignored, if not positively condemned.

No, the true work of advanced spirits is better accomplished by the employment of instruments that *are born and trained in the schools of experience and adversity.* These have had no time to foster pride and indolence in their youth; and, by the time that maturity is attained, the disposition to indulge in such dissipation as these conditions foster is past danger of indulgence.

It seems to the world strange that this should be so, but the truth is that the power of intelligent spirits to produce results through manipulation of the brain organism gives them almost omnipotent control over the mortal realm; and they are exercising this knowledge at the present time in a manner that is bringing the world forward in the lines of true growth, so that one generation now achieves more than ten did five centuries ago.

This is the triumph of science and scientific methods in dealing with the problems of mortal and spiritual existence. The world can choose between the religious and scientific modes of thought, but it must not complain if it chooses the former that it remains a laggard in the race, that must be as long as life shall be generated upon the planet. Under the religious influence the mind tends towards crystallization, or the inorganic forms of elemental expression of forces. Under the scientific it grows and expands in its powers until, like a gigantic organism, it embraces within its arms the universe of matter, and becomes almost, if not quite, what Plato meant when he pictured it as a possibility of human attainment, viz., "A perfect Intelligence worthy of Divine honors, if Divine honors are worthy of bestowal upon any Intelligence whatever," which I, for one, should seriously question from the knowledge I have of spiritual life, and which none desire who have advanced to the standard of Plato's delineation.

www.ingramcontent.com/pod-product-compliance
Lightning Source LLC
Chambersburg PA
CBHW031449270326
41930CB00007B/917